All Beer and Sk

A Short History of Inns and Ta

ED GIBBONS

The National Trust

FOR DAAVE

ACKNOWLEDGEMENTS

I have many people to thank for their help with the research and writing of this book
– landlords, landladies and their regulars, work colleagues, family and friends –
but particularly Emily, for her love and support,
and Helen and Margaret for their guidance and encouragement.

First published in Great Britain in 2001 by the National Trust (Enterprises) Ltd
36 Queen Anne's Gate, London SW1H 9AS
www.nationaltrust.org.uk/bookshop
Registered charity no. 205846

ISBN 0 7078 0297 0
A catalogue record for this book is available from the British Library

Picture research by Ed Gibbons and Helen Fewster
Designed and typeset by Peter and Alison Guy
Production by Chris Pearson
Printed in Italy by G. Canale & C.S.p.A

Front cover: The bar at the Crown Liquor Saloon in Belfast.
Back cover: *The Card Players* by Alfred Gilbert, 1875, from Sunnycroft in Shropshire.
Title page: *A Butler Carrying Ale*, watercolour from Powis Castle in Wales.

Introduction

From the towns all inns have been driven; from the villages most....
Change your hearts or you will lose your inns and you will deserve to have
lost them. But when you have lost your inns drown your empty selves for
you will have lost the last of England.

Hilaire Belloc 'On Inns' *This and That* (1912)

Hilaire Belloc's melancholy observation gives the impression that there were no more
than a handful of inns left in early twentieth-century Britain, and even these had little
chance of survival. Equally despondent was Frederick Hackwood, who, in his *Inns, Ales
and Drinking Customs of Old England* (1909), complained about the arrival of 'perpendicular drinking' and the degenerative British habit of buying rounds. Even today,
people are bemoaning the passing of 'real inns' as chains of identical pubs sweep all
before them. But although large open spaces full of pine and wine may not be every-
body's idea of fun, they are no more than the next step in the development of inns and
drinking, and no doubt in time will be replaced by the next fashion.

Change and development mean life remains interesting and inns are no less a part of
this than anything else – perhaps more so, considering their place at the hub of the community. For centuries they have reflected life in its many guises. They have been at the
heart of legislation – on both sides of the bar – for longer than landlords and late-night
drinkers would care to remember. They have developed alongside changes in transport,
responded to the needs of tourism and adapted to the advances made possible by the
Industrial Revolution. Some have rumbled along at the gentle pace of village life, whilst
others have bustled day and night for hundreds of years in the city centre.

This ability to change, to keep abreast of progress, reinforces the idea that inns are simply a microcosm of goings-on in the wider world, steeped in social history and brim full
of stories confirming that fact is stranger than fiction. These anecdotes, intertwined with
the development of drinking and inns, show us that the inn like all British institutions
has adapted and developed over the centuries and is certainly not in demise.

Early Rounds

It is impossible to pin-point exactly when the first alehouse originated, but it is known that Britons were drinking alcoholic beverages long before the Romans arrived. Ale has been the British drink of choice ever since Phoenician traders first brought barley – and brewing – to Europe, and it is now widely believed amongst scholars that thousands of years ago man ceased his nomadic lifestyle to plant grain not for baking, as traditionally thought, but for brewing. So in 55 B C, when the terrifying sight of Julius Caesar's fleet was first seen advancing towards Britain, it is highly likely that onlookers knew exactly where to go to calm their nerves.

But it was the Romans, with their genius for organisation, who established the first roadside *tavernae* to provide refreshment for the troops patrolling the country. The chequer boards hanging at their entrances indicated that these were places to eat, drink, exchange money and conduct business, and the locals soon took to them, even if they weren't so impressed by the wine. Taverns were therefore well established by the time the Vikings turned up in the late eighth century and, with their legendary love of *ol* (ale), they no doubt strengthened the general drinking powers of the inhabitants, and contributed to the development of the national beverages of mead and ale.

Their Norman cousins who came to England with William the Conqueror likewise did little to change the way we drank: attempts to introduce wine and regulate drinking habits consistently failed to have any effect. Indeed, until the regular availability of clean drinking water in the nineteenth century, ale was a dietary staple for all times of day providing sustenance and acting as a thirst quencher, pain-killer and prophylactic. A beer allowance was part of the pay packet from the fourteenth century until the Victorians put a stop to it, and prices were protected by law to ensure that even the poor man could afford his ale.

By the Middle Ages every household used yeast to bake and brew simultaneously. The best brewsters (invariably women) would share their creation with their neighbours and would signal the arrival of a new brew by sticking a pole out of the window with some sort of foliage attached – an early form of the inn-sign issuing an invitation to enter. This sharing of the produce encouraged the development of the village inn and it soon became the hub of the community, the place for people to meet and socialise.

A Village Fair attributed to Luke Clennell (1781–1840). Scenes from village life have always been popular subjects for paintings, and many faithfully depict the inn at the centre of events. Here the inn-sign, showing a blue bell, is prominently displayed ensuring that fair-goers would know where to find refreshment.

The Centre of the Community

Understandably, as people gravitated towards those who produced the most satisfying ale, the homes of the best brewers eventually emerged as the local alehouses. Village inns have therefore experienced hotchpotch development. The Bankes Arms in Studland in Dorset, for instance, which became an inn in the nineteenth century, is based around an old cottage that is thought to be at least four hundred years old.

In Ireland it is still common to find small bars that are little more than the landlord's front room. Often you can find the village shop there too, also run by the landlord. However Mary McBride's

bar in the fishing village of Cushendun, Co. Antrim, does not offer this service – and for a good reason. The front bar, which has only in recent years been joined by a back room and adjoining dining rooms, is reputedly the smallest in Ireland. Once inside, to say three is a crowd might be an exaggeration, but four is definitely cosy.

These days it is rare to find such intimacy in urban pubs, but in small rural communities the inn as the thriving social centre is still very much alive. The village tavern has often been the logical place to meet and conduct business transactions, though these have not always been quite as one might have expected. The minutes for the parish vestry meetings, held in the Church Loft across the road from the George and Dragon in West Wycombe in Buckinghamshire, reveal that the gatherings often adjourned to the inn. But in 1762, enough was enough and it was minuted that 'all business shall be done in the Church Loft and the Books shall never be carried to a Publick House'.

In 1938 the Nelson's Head in Horsey, Norfolk, found itself quite literally at the centre of events. The sea defences were so badly breached that nearly the whole area was under water for three months. The only place that remained dry, so to speak, was the inn, sitting on a slightly raised piece of ground. It served as a place to go and bond over the disaster and where the local postman could relax after his delivery round, which involved rowing fifteen miles a day when the waters were up.

Mary McBride's bar in the village of Cushendun, Northern Ireland, and, opposite, the tiny tap-room which perhaps takes intimacy to new extremes. The bar is reputedly the smallest in Ireland.

Inns have served as polling stations, banks, concert venues, theatres, courtrooms and post offices. They have been places to go to look for work, read the paper, watch a live sporting event or play a game. When very few people had access to legal expertise, peripatetic lawyers could be found at inns offering advice to quizzical locals. The same locals returned there on pay day and, more begrudgingly, on rent day. Visitors might find themselves the subject of an animated attempt by a politician to win their vote, no doubt by being plied with drink and food. Or they might opt for a quiet haircut with their pint – the danger being that they would then provide a captive audience for the witterings of the pub bore.

The diversity to be found today in Britain's country taverns reflects the fact that much of their development has been dictated by events – whether the village was on a coaching route, near a beauty spot, sporting facilities or a seaside resort, or well placed to profit from industrial development. Although the Tower Bank Arms in Near Sawrey in Cumbria offered a focal point for the local farmers, it was one resident who was directly responsible for the inn's subsequent trade. Beatrix Potter may have taken part in avid discussions about her prize-winning Herdwick sheep at the farmers' meetings in the inn, but it was the appearance of the Tower Bank Arms as a small country inn in *The Tale of Jemima Puddleduck* that brought in the visitors. The inn backs on to Beatrix Potter's farm, Hill Top, and tourists often pop in for a swift half after visiting the property.

The Tower Bank Arms in Near Sawrey, Cumbria, painted by Beatrix Potter to illustrate *The Tale of Jemima Puddleduck*.

Entertainment

Life ain't all beer and skittles, and more's the pity;
but what's the odds so long as you're happy?
George du Maurier, *Trilby* (1894)

Throughout the ages, inns and alehouses have been the place to go to be entertained, although the form it has taken has changed enormously since the days when Geoffrey Chaucer set the Tabard Inn in Southwark as the start of a pilgrimage to Canterbury. Bear-baiting and cock-fighting were superseded by more genteel pastimes like boxing. 'The noble art' has a long association with inns, not least because that was where fights were originally staged.

For those who didn't appreciate two men trying to knock the living daylights out of each other, more refined games have been available. The Privy Purse records show that Henry VIII was a keen, if erratic, shove ha'penny player, whose regular losses were a source of gossip at Court. On one occasion in 1532, 'Lord William won £9 of the King at Shouvilla Bourde'; fortunately the King's fortunes changed in the next games he played and he won £45 from Lord Rochford, Anne Boleyn's brother. Darts were played on *The Mayflower*'s voyage to the New World in 1620, and dominoes were introduced by French prisoners whiling away their captivity during the Napoleonic Wars.

The business of using a ball to strike an object has many variants. Skittles have been hugely popular over the centuries, and although the game has now developed into ten-pin bowling, it seems unlikely that the phrase 'It's not all beer and ten-pin bowling' will ever really catch on. Francis Drake's preferred pastime of bowls is still around, but the table versions of billiards (all the rage in pubs in the 1890s), snooker and pool are now more popular.

For those who didn't want to compete, but just preferred singing and dancing, inns have always provided somewhere for a knees-up. An inventory at the Hardwick Inn in Derbyshire listed a pair of virginals in 1647 and such was the popularity of concerts upstairs in pubs during the nineteenth century that it spawned the whole music-hall culture. Pub-singers and bands still thrive, as do their impromptu warbling karaoke cousins.

The Card Players by David Teniers the Younger (1610–1690) from Polesden Lacey in Surrey. There are a number of tavern scenes in the collection; Polesden Lacey was the home of Mrs Ronald Greville, daughter of the self-made millionaire brewer William McEwan. She was refreshingly candid about her background, and once famously remarked, 'I would rather be a beeress than a peeress'.

The Coaching Era

Improving roads and better methods of transport caused village inns on the main routes to develop quite differently from their more remote counterparts. The Turnpike Acts of 1663 encouraged the paving of roads and thus people to travel more. Accommodation, extensive yards, stabling and storage – not to mention refreshment – were needed at the points of departure and arrival, as were regular places to change the horses and even more frequent spots to water them along the way. Public stagecoaches followed given routes, transporting goods and mail as well as passengers, so coaching inns were established and life revolved around the comings and goings of the next mailcoach.

A map of Southwark *c.*1542 shows several inns by name including the George, which suggests that it had long been a popular spot for travellers coming up to London. Like many inns, it acted as a delivery point for goods purchased in the City, which were then sent on to their country destinations – an early example of the convenience of home delivery. The George was well equipped with extensive stabling; fashionable galleries provided access to the guestrooms and it became an important departure point southwards. The interior panelling, which dates from the eighteenth century, shows that it prospered, and by the early nineteenth century it catered for nearly one-fifth of the carriers using Southwark inns. At least seven coaches and a dozen wagons and endless carts and gigs, would go in and out of the two yards all day long.

The exterior of the George Inn in Southwark. Galleried inns of this kind were once extremely fashionable, but there were very practical reasons for adopting this style – the building backed onto others, and this was the easiest way to ensure that the bedrooms had windows.

In order to maintain their speed, coaches would stop approximately every eight to ten miles to change horses at posts, as they were known across Europe. This meant that well-placed villages would be visited on a regular basis. West Wycombe in Buckinghamshire, on the routes from London to Oxford and Aylesbury, thrived so much so that at one stage it boasted four inns, all serving the coaching industry, including the George and Dragon. The pub is an imposing brick building that towers over the rest of the street as a result of an extensive rebuild *c.*1720, which encased the earlier inn and added stables, accommodation and quite possibly the spectacular lead sign depicting the legend of St George and his dragon. Made of solid lead, it declared the wealth of the place – as if that was necessary, with an ostentatious façade in such humble surroundings. This expansion and display of wealth shows that some seventy years prior to the peak of the coaching era, canny innkeepers were predicting that traffic was going to increase, and were already developing their facilities to cope with it.

With the constant stream of travellers to and from London, the George and Dragon witnessed all sorts of shenanigans over the years, but the best-known tale is also the most tragic. A local serving girl at the inn called Sukie, keen to escape the confines of village life, fell for the charms of a gentleman customer and arranged to meet him at the dead of night and elope. But he never showed up – it was a joke played by the local boys who were jealous that Sukie thought herself above them. As she fled, humiliated, she tripped, fell and later died from her injuries at the inn, where, it is said, she still makes the occasional appearance.

Stagecoaches travelling between main change-over points would still need to stop to water the horses – not to mention the postilions – at regular intervals. The 'Lord Exmouth', which ran 100 miles between Lancaster and Newcastle, would start its journey at 4.00a.m., pausing at the Cross Keys in Cautley in Cumbria to water man and beast before going on to Kirby Stephen to change horses and continue to its destination, arriving at about 7.30p.m. On one trip, whilst the two coachmen were partaking of something warming at the Cross Keys, the horses were startled and set off along the road. A young gentleman who had been aboard and was stretching his legs, leapt on a spare horse and gave chase. But he failed to calm the horses and was thrown off. By the time he and the coachmen caught up with it, the vehicle was sitting outside its next stop in Kirby Stephen. In the back a young couple were still fast asleep – oblivious that they had just travelled another ten miles totally unaccompanied.

The Traveller's Breakfast by Edward Villiers Rippingille, 1824, features several literary figures including Dorothy and William Wordsworth, Charles Lamb, Robert Southey and Samuel Coleridge gathered at an inn while their coachman shivers on his box outside the window.

The Rise of the Railway Tavern

In the nineteenth century, the railway boom spelt the end for the coaching inn but spawned the rise of the railway tavern. As many coaching inns crashed out of business some were ironically rescued by the very railway companies that they were competing against. In Southwark, the George was saved when its yards and outbuildings were occupied by a railway company using nearby London Bridge station. Its future was further secured in 1878 when Amelia Murray and her daughter, Agnes, took over. Together they ran the inn for over fifty years, happily embellishing the rumour that Charles Dickens was a regular, and fostering the George's reputation as an 'ancient inn of England' by stubbornly refusing to modernise – a bathroom was not installed until after Agnes' death in 1934. As a result historical and literary societies came to visit, plays were staged in the yard and an endless stream of tourists arrived, including Winston Churchill, who was rude enough to bring his own port and was duly charged 1s 6d corkage.

The railway boom was also responsible for the development of an ordinary village inn, the Bankes Arms Hotel at Corfe Castle in Dorset. People have been passing through Corfe Castle for centuries: in earlier times masons and quarrymen on their way to and from the quarries of Purbeck and Portland stone, later, tourists coming to see the spectacular ruined castle, or en route to Swanage and other seaside resorts on the Isle of Purbeck. Before the railways were developed in the 1880s there was an established inn here, offering accommodation and stabling to visitors. But the railway changed the inn's fortunes – not to mention its name. Originally known as the Ship Inn, it went through two or three variations before settling on its present name in deference to its long-time owners, the Bankes family. Set up as a commercial hotel proper, incorporating a postal service, it underwent considerable modernisation to satisfy the influx of visitors stepping off the train at the bottom of the garden.

Thanks to the railway the Tyn y Groes, on its perch above the Mawddach River in Gwynedd, became a viable resort for those wishing to enjoy the quality fishing. In the nineteenth century, William Gladstone was a regular visitor, always taking the same room overlooking the best spot on the river, so that as soon as he awoke he could see if the conditions were right. Unfortunately on one visit he got involved in a blazing row with his son over Home Rule in Ireland – the discussion was overheard by other visitors and the issue eventually led to the fall of his Liberal Government.

In the early twentieth century the Tyn y Groes (meaning house by the crossroads) became part of a chain run by Quellyn Roberts & Co, who catered for the upper end of the market. An old brochure advertised 3s 6d for a double room, a further 3s for the pleasure of a private sitting room and the not insignificant sum of 6s per accompanying member of staff. But for those visitors who wondered if they were getting their money's worth, the brochure also informed them that 'the water supplies and sanitary arrangements have been fully renewed', which must have come as some relief, given that the body of the inn dates from the eighteenth century, or before.

The interior of the George in Southwark retains its simplicity today – wooden chairs and tables preserve the ambience of an ancient inn. The fine eighteenth-century panelling dates from the George's prosperous days in the coaching era.

SOUTHWARK BAR

THE GEORGE
EST. 1676.
FAMOUS
ALES, PORTERS & STOUTS
IN PERFECT CONDITION
TARIFF

REPUTED PINTS

Finest Ale	4ᵈ
Mulled Ale	4½ᵈ
Special Strong Ale	5ᵈ
Porter + Stout	3ᵈ
Norfolk Cyder	3ᵈ

Estate Inns

Just as village inns emerged to serve the needs of the community, so wealthy landowners recognised the need to provide alehouses for their workers. The Buckinghamshire Arms, on the Blickling Estate in Norfolk, was originally built as a house for the estate bricklayer in the seventeenth century. Soon after completion, it was operating as an alehouse.

The Hardwick Inn, at the gates of Hardwick Hall in Derbyshire, was built at the end of the sixteenth century in tandem with that extravagant prodigy house by Elizabeth, Countess of Shrewsbury, better known as Bess of Hardwick. Prodigy houses were intended to display wealth, and true to form Hardwick New Hall sits on top of a hill and is adorned all around the roofline with Bess's initials 'ES' for Elizabeth Shrewsbury and her Countess's coronet. Bess was an avid and experienced builder, well aware that her workforce and tenants would appreciate their smart new inn, built under the auspices of the painter, John Ballechouse, who was in charge of the decorating operations at Hardwick.

But legend has it that there was more to Bess's relentless building than the desire to broadcast her wealth: a soothsayer reputedly told Bess that she would die if she ever stopped her building work. For over twenty years she refurbished Hardwick Old Hall then, on the death of her fourth husband, promptly started on the New Hall. In the winter of 1607/8 the mortar was mixed with ale, which has a lower freezing point, to keep it set – common practice in the Middle Ages. However the extreme severity of the weather in that season meant that not even hot ale would make the cement set and building work ground to a halt. The consequences were fatal for Bess, who died of a chill early in the New Year.

Both the Buckinghamshire Arms and the Hardwick Inn were an integral part of their estates, but they also provided accommodation. Within fifty years of completion, the Buckinghamshire Arms was extended with the addition of Flemish-style gables and a stable block to cope with increasing numbers of visitors. The Hardwick Inn, however, was better prepared and needed hardly any renovation for 250 years: the inventory of 1647 records that it was furnished with 'Bedding ffurniture etc, fitting for the entertainment of gentlemen and strangers'.

But not even Bess could have predicted quite how strange the visitors would become. During the Second World War the clientele of both inns extended to include army and R.A.F. officers who were stationed in the houses. The Buckinghamshire Arms was particularly popular, and many officers returned there after the war. Among the signatures in the visitors' book in the bar is that of the legless war hero, Douglas Bader.

The imposing exterior of Hardwick Hall in Derbyshire, and the Hardwick
Inn (facing page), which was built for the tenants living on the estate.

Tourism

Unlike the Buckinghamshire Arms and the Hardwick Inn, the Spread Eagle on the estate at Stourhead in Wiltshire was built specifically for the benefit of tourists. Stourhead House was rebuilt in 1717 in the fashionable Palladian style by Colen Campbell for the banker Henry Hoare I. His son, also called Henry, filled it with art and furniture collected on the European Grand Tour, and then proceeded to landscape his estate, creating one of the world's great gardens. Within the natural landscape of lakes and woods, he set temples and other buildings as 'eye-catchers' to summon up a living version of the ideal classical paintings of Claude or Poussin. From the outset, Henry Hoare II intended his garden to be open to visitors, 'the Gentleman' who would appreciate the cultural associations as they came upon the various features. But the sheer beauty of the garden also appealed to what he described as 'the Vulgar', who came in large numbers.

The Spread Eagle, taking the Eagle from the Hoare coat of arms, was built as a direct response to the popularity of the gardens. But, as Mrs Lybbe Powys discovered in 1765, you had to be quick if you wanted refreshment or accommodation. In her diary, she recorded: 'We intended staying at the inn at Stourton, built by Mr. Hoare for the company that comes to see his place, but to our mortification, when we got there at ten o'clock, it was full, and we were obliged to go on to Mere.'

The inn remained popular with tourists, many of whom recorded their visits by scratching their names on the bar-room window. One of the more recent additions was made by the actor, David Niven, and his wife. Niven used to drink at the Spread Eagle when he was based nearby during the Second World War. In 1941, his wife joined him for a visit from London, and they commemorated their tryst with a joint inscription on the window.

North-west view of the inn at Stourton, watercolour by J.C. Buckler, (1817), at Stourhead in Wiltshire.

Tourism grew during the nineteenth century and was indirectly responsible for the survival of another National Trust pub with maritime connections. Early in the nineteenth century the village of Porthdinllaen in North Wales held a strong case for developing into the main port for commercial shipping to Ireland. The wide natural harbour had over 600 ships docking a year and was a centre for shipbuilding, quarrying and herring fishing. In anticipation of the new port, property developers moved in and their activities included the slightly premature construction of a hotel. But in 1819 the village's growth was arrested by Parliament's decision to develop the harbour at Holyhead instead. Legend has it that the village lost out by just one vote and it is darkly maintained that the geological samples that swung the deal actually came from Porthdinllaen.

The Ty Coch Inn was built from red brick ballast (Ty Coch means 'red house') at around the time of the new port proposals. Originally intended as a vicarage for the village of Edern three miles away, the building became Porthdinllaen's third inn after Edern gained a more accessible vicarage. Despite catering almost exclusively for tourists – only four or five working boats make use of the harbour nowadays – it is still a popular local, and has outlasted the other two inns.

One visiting sailor certainly made his mark. Having

docked his boat in the bay one winter he proceeded to draw too much attention to himself with an excessive use – especially in such an isolated location – of £50 notes. The locals quickly suspected he was on the wrong side of the law, although he was not one of the Brinks Matt Bullion robbers as they had hoped. Nevertheless the style of his final capture was highly dramatic, as he was chased over the dunes by the local bobby on a motorised tricycle.

Today, the interior of the Ty Coch Inn reflects not only its maritime associations but also a long-standing habit of many landlords and landladies over the centuries –

the display of personal collections. Collections have varied in taste and quality, ranging from stuffed animals to sporting memorabilia, from fossils to neck ties. The present incumbent at the Ty Coch Inn has spent more than thirty years building up an extraordinary collection of tankards and lamps, including a pair of train lamps that are rumoured to have once lit up the Queen's train – before it stopped a little too long in Crewe Station.

The bright red brick of the Ty Coch Inn in the fishing village of Porthdinllaen, is clearly visible across the sheltered harbour.

Mine Host

Who ran these inns? In villages, some inns have remained in the same families for years. The Vine Inn at Pamphill in Dorset, for instance, has been presided over by one family since it was granted a licence *c.*1900, and likewise the Swan at West Wycombe, run by generations of the same family since 1910. Retired sportsmen and soldiers have often opted for a complete change of lifestyle and set up as landlords. One such was Sergeant William Lawrence, batman to Captain 'kiss me' Hardy, who left the navy with a distinguished service record and arrived in Studland Bay to set up a tavern which he rather strangely named after the Duke of Wellington rather than Admiral Nelson. This well-connected stranger was granted the first royal licence in the area, which might well have caused panic among the locals in an area renowned for smuggling.

On estates, it was not uncommon for the landowner to appoint one of their faithful employees to the position. Bess of Hardwick not only entrusted John Ballechouse with the building of the Hardwick Inn, but appointed him as the first tenant on its completion. The Marquises of Lothian, owners of Blickling in the nineteenth century, were less fortunate in their selection of a landlord. In 1835 Algernon Alfred Bloss was evicted from the Buckinghamshire Arms with debts of over £210 – which amounted to at least four years' rent. The Lothians' run of bad luck continued, for after only six years the tenancy was up for grabs again. The equally magnificently named Theophilus Wells, who succeeded Bloss, died in the job: the coroner's report simply referred to the cause of death as 'liver'.

Just how highly tenancies were valued is revealed by a tragic incident at Dolaucothi in Pumpsaint, South Wales. The estate had been the domain of the Johnes family since the sixteenth century, and in the nineteenth century was presided over by the widely respected Judge John Johnes, Recorder of Carmarthen. In 1876 the position of landlord at the Dolaucothi Arms became vacant, and Johnes' loyal butler, Tremble, asked if, after seventeen years' service, he might leave and apply for the job. It is not known why the Judge refused his request, but the butler was devastated. Taking a shotgun to the library, Tremble shot Johnes dead as he sat in his chair.

Mine workings on the Dolaucothi Estate in Carmarthenshire. Had Tremble been successful in his application to run the Dolaucothi Arms in Pumpsaint, he could quite literally have found himself sitting on a gold mine: it is possible that the inn's cellars were once used by the Romans to store their gold.

Brewing

As a dietary staple in the Middle Ages ale was in great demand, and that other centre of the community, the Church, brewed on a massive scale. Monks provided both for their own needs, for their lay brothers, and for the pilgrims who came to visit. The Domesday Book records that the monks of St Paul's Cathedral in London produced 67,814 gallons (1,884 barrels) of ale made from barley, wheat and oats each year. In the twelfth century, the vast brewhouse at the Cistercian monastery of Fountains Abbey in Yorkshire housed an operation capable of producing sixty barrels of strong ale every ten days. Irish missionaries carried their expertise across Europe – the Benedictine abbey founded by St Gall in what is now Switzerland had a thriving brewing business in the ninth century, and Germany later boasted 505 brewing monasteries.

Many country houses had their own brewhouses as, like the monasteries, landowners supported communities of servants and estate workers in addition to the household. One of the most complete and earliest examples survives at Lacock Abbey in Wiltshire. Lacock was originally an Augustinian nunnery, suppressed by Henry VIII in 1539 and converted to a private house by Sir William Sharington. The brewhouse probably dates from this period rather than from its convent days, and still has its mash tun, cooling trough and fermenting vat.

Other examples of brewhouses, such as that at Charlecote Park in Warwickshire, date from the eighteenth century, when the number of private brewhouses grew rapidly. In 1830 it was calculated that country-house breweries accounted for over twenty per cent of the beer produced in Britain. They varied little in design, which was not surprising since the brewing techniques themselves had changed little over the centuries. Brewers would pass their knowledge on from one generation to the next to produce consistently a reasonably good brew and ensure the regular delivery of a staple. For these reasons, there was little room for experimentation, nor was it encouraged in the rigid formality of the country house.

Nowadays only Hickleton in Yorkshire (not NT) survives with an original functioning brewhouse, although Shugborough in Staffordshire has carried out major renovations and occasionally brews its own Shugborough Ale.

View of the sixteenth-century brewery at Lacock Abbey in Wiltshire. After boiling in the copper (left) the liquid would run into the shallow cooling trough and then into the vat beneath it, ready for fermentation.

The Law

Over-indulgence in alcohol has been a perennial problem. Four thousand years ago in Egyptian Pelusium, a renowned centre of both learning and brewing, a reformer was calling for control on the number of alehouses in the city. But a thousand years later the city suffered from the familiar problem of students neglecting their studies in favour of drinking.

Attempts at regulation have been on-going, with the Romans keeping their houses in order in Britain, while the Anglo-Saxon King of Kent, Ethelbert, was trying to regulate the 'eala-hus' in 616. A significant advance was made in 1267 with Henry III's Assize of Bread and Ale, which regulated price and quality. Ale-conners were appointed across the country to check that standards were adhered to and that the beer was served in the correct amounts (false-bottomed vessels were common). This was a respected post and one that Nicholas Cobb, landlord, brewer and blacksmith at the Bankes Arms in Corfe Castle, was appointed to in 1691. One of his tasks is likely to have been to check the ale for added sugar, a common brewers' practice in the seventeenth century to try to salvage sour beer. Ale-conners would enter an inn wearing their traditional leather trousers, pour some beer onto a seat and sit in it for thirty minutes. If they could rise afterwards, all was well, but if the ale had extra sugar in it, they would get stuck and have to reprimand the landlord. There cannot have been a shortage of comic instances on these occasions, as the officer struggled to separate himself from his seat whilst trying

seriously to address the landlord.

The 1552 Licensing Act represents a watershed in licensing laws as, for the first time, it brought inns in England and Wales under state control. Once inns were thus controlled, more time could be spent in protecting the consumer from excessive drunkenness – and punishing them for it. The George Inn in the village of Lacock found itself in the dock for offences on both sides of the bar. In 1610 the innkeeper 'David Weste of Laycocke' appeared in front of the authorities charged with staging unlawful games 'that is to say tables cards and shuffleboards and also drunkenness and other misdemeanours'. And he was not the only one. There was more trouble in 1656 when two blaspheming weavers were pulled in front of the Grand Jury. One claimed 'that there was noe Christ but the sun that shines upon us', whilst the other believed God was omni-present and hence if the weaver himself was drunk, then 'god was drunke with him'.

Being pulled up for blaspheming is perhaps a little ironic as church-ales (ale in this context means a festival – there were also Easter-ales and Christening-ales) were widespread and drunkenness at them was common. The behaviour of the local vicar in Yeovil in Somerset, who was put in the stocks for being drunk in 1502, might sound a little unexceptional until we learn that he was Thomas Wolsey, the future Cardinal and Archbishop of York.

The George Inn at Lacock in Wiltshire. Records show that it has one of the longest continually held licences in the West Country.

Legislation in 1604 stipulated that only those staying overnight at an inn were permitted to drink there, leaving the locals very much out in the cold with the predictable result that unlicensed houses sprang up all over the place. Punishments for 'tippling townsmen' were a 3s 4d payment to the poor, or five hours in the stocks. This was soon increased to 5s or six hours of public humiliation. This rise in the punishment perhaps suggests that not enough people were being deterred. In fact between 1604 and 1627 there were no less than seven Acts of Parliament attempting to control drunkenness – but with no obvious success.

As King Charles I struggled to raise money in his quarrels with Parliament, duty on beer duly rose. Restrictions were also placed on foreign imports of brandy and other spirits though the distilling of home-grown gin was encouraged. Cheap, potent and addictive gin created havoc in no time, sending many a mother to their ruin. Only the advent of the Temperance Movement in the nineteenth century finally reversed the situation, with duty on wholesome British beer being lowered and that on gin raised. As further support, beer licenses became readily available to all and sundry at two guineas (£2 2s) apiece, whilst spirit licenses had to be gained from a magistrate. The idea was noble but in practice it never worked as Victorian property developers were happy to bribe magistrates to get the full licences that they wanted.

The eighteenth-century dog wheel is one of the most remarkable features to be seen at the George in Lacock. Once commonplace, they are now a rare sight. A special breed of dog, a turnspit, would run inside the wheel, rotating the spit in the fireplace. Among the every day phrases commemorating this practice are 'it's a dog's life', 'dog tired' and possibly 'dog's nose' – a drink of beer mixed with rum or gin that may have been a reward for a tired dog, or fuel to keep the poor thing running.

Perpendicular Drinking

The individuality and style of the Crown Liquor Saloon may have been excessive even by late nineteenth-century standards, but it provided everything the Victorian pub-goer could wish for: opportunities for secluded intimacy in the snugs, enclosed by screens of wood faced with coloured glass, combined with plenty of space for general conviviality at the long, curving bar.

However, the advent of such counter service gave Frederick Hackwood cause for concern as patrons could be served quicker and drink faster while standing up. Traditionally innkeepers had allowed their guests to spend the evening over a single jug of beer if they so wished. But in his book Hackwood remarks that, particularly in urban gin palaces, 'the repeated order is the condition of a continued welcome. This attitude of the management is betrayed by the inhospitable seatless bar, specially designed for "perpendicular drinking".'

Hackwood's worry was that people were thus encouraged to drink far more than they needed to. The situation was compounded by the time-honoured but 'irksome' English custom of 'treating another person to drinks' that would take 'some moral courage to resist':

> It is the English practice of all others which is characteristically stupid, in that it leads to unnecessary drinking; for a meeting of friends on the common ground of a public-house is invariably celebrated by their drinking together, and, as a rule, an end cannot be put to the celebration till each man has acquitted himself by paying for 'drinks round' – and therefore the larger the party the larger the number of drinks taken, and probably all of them except the first quite unnecessary, either for the quenching of thirst or the celebration of a happy meeting.

The bar at the Crown Liquor Saloon in Belfast is decorated with patterned tiles. The concave shape reveals that it was designed for the comfort of those patrons who preferred to drink sitting down, although Hackwood is unlikely to have approved.

What's in a name?

The Crown Liquor Saloon not only has an interesting beginning (see pages 41 and 43), but its name also carries a story. Tradition has it that the landlord Michael Flanagan was an Irish Nationalist, and his wife a Loyalist. She stamped her mark on the pub by insisting it was called the Crown. However, Flanagan made his point by depicting a crown in mosaics at the front door, so that those wishing to wipe their feet on it could do so.

The names of inns and pubs have been inspired by all sorts of extraordinary things – many lost in history – which have been the subject of a number of books and even more bar-room discussions. The most popular group seems to be those named after royalty and national heroes, whether they be inspired by loyalty, admiration, or even a chance visit. The heads and arms of Kings and Queens may be found all over the country – not to mention their crowns. George II, the last British monarch to lead his troops into battle, inspired a few christenings in his own right, including Lacock's George Inn. The legendary saint is another George popular on inn signs, often depicted slaying the dragon, as at West Wycombe. A true national hero who has had many an inn named in his honour is Admiral Lord Nelson. The Nelson's Head in Horsey in Norfolk, the Admiral's home county, is by no means alone in claiming he stopped off there once – and it is not unlikely that he relieved himself, as the legend claims.

Heraldic symbols and religious connections also give rise to many names – such as the Spread Eagle at Stourton, which is part of the Hoare family's coat of arms, and the Red Lion, a popular heraldic image, at Bradenham in Buckinghamshire. In religious paintings saints have always had traditional symbols to help the illiterate identify them – and inns happily copied this symbolism. So it is of little surprise that at Cautley we find the Cross Keys, the attribute of St Peter, keeper of the doors to Heaven.

The exterior of the Crown Liquor Saloon is suitably impressive with its classical pilasters and portico supported by cast iron columns. A mosaic crown is carefully positioned on the floor at the entrance.

But pub names can be bizarre. There is a widely held belief that straightforward religious connections have led, through bastardisation over the centuries, to some of the more unlikely inn names. The Goat and Compasses is thought to have derived from the phrase 'God Encompasseth Us' whilst the Cat and Fiddle originates from *Catherine Fidelis*. However, the varied opinions on the origin of the Pig and Whistle that I have come across have left me too confused to voice any of them – but they seem to have had little to do with animals.

The Fleece Inn by contrast, no doubt took its name from its farming past, whilst the Old Dungeon Ghyll named itself after the local tourist attraction and the reason for its existence – the Dungeon Ghyll waterfall. But here it is the prefix that is interesting. It was common for a new inn to take the name of a successful local establishment in an attempt to attract custom, causing the latter to add the prefix 'Old' or 'Original' to differentiate them. For the Old Dungeon Ghyll to have to add the prefix within only four or five years of establishment indicates an extraordinarily popular area.

Nowadays it is unlikely that new pubs will follow the name of a local rival to try to steal their custom. Rather, they will be part of a chain with the same theme and identical décor. Modern names, especially in towns and cities, are more likely to be a clever pun than reflective of a traditional sign. Some say the advent of pub chains means that the traditional inn is dying out, but it strikes me more as a natural development. Inns and pubs have always adapted to meet the needs of society and repetitive chain pubs reflect the modern preference to be somewhere new, yet familiar. But it is for this very reason, the comfort of familiarity, that the traditional British pub and inn will always remain. As that inveterate patron of taverns Dr Johnson so cannily observed: 'There is nothing which has yet been contrived by man by which so much happiness has been produced as by a good tavern or inn.'

The inn-sign of the George in Southwark.

Inns and Public Houses owned by The National Trust

BERKSHIRE
Radnor Arms, Coleshill

BUCKINGHAMSHIRE
King's Head, Aylesbury
Red Lion, Bradenham
George & Dragon, West Wycombe
Old Plough, West Wycombe
Swan, West Wycombe

CHESHIRE
Wizard of the Edge, Alderley Edge
    (now restaurant only)

CUMBRIA
Cross Keys, Cautley
Old Dungeon Ghyll, Great Langdale
Strickland Arms, Sizergh
Tower Bank Arms, Near Sawrey

DERBYSHIRE
Hardwick Inn, nr Chesterfield

DEVON
Red Lion, Broadclyst
Marisco Tavern, Lundy

DORSET
Bankes Arms Hotel, Corfe Castle
Vine Inn, Pamphill
Bankes Arms, Studland
Manor House Hotel, Studland

KENT
Castle Inn, Chiddingstone

LONDON
George Inn, Southwark

NORFOLK
Buckinghamshire Arms, Blickling
Nelson's Head, Horsey

NORTHUMBERLAND
Ship Inn, Low Newton-by-the-Sea

SUSSEX
Castle Inn, Bodiam

WILTSHIRE
Red Lion, Kilmington
George Inn, Lacock
Red Lion, Lacock
Sign of the Angel, Lacock
    (now restaurant and hotel only)
Spread Eagle, Stourton

WORCESTERSHIRE
Fleece Inn, Bretforton

CARMARTHENSHIRE
Cwmdu Inn, Cwmdu
Dolaucothi Arms, Pumpsaint

GWYNEDD
Tyn-y-Groes, Ganllwyd
Ty Coch Inn, Porthdinllaen

NORTHERN IRELAND
Crown Liquor Saloon, Belfast, Co. Antrim
Mary McBride's, Cushendun, Co. Antrim